Poems by
An Old Fenman
Lew Gray

This one for Mother:

Many are your acts of loving care
Absolute unselfish acts of love
Regardless of the pain, your fingers bare
Your providence attained without a glove
Generosity has been your trait
Regardless of your problems, come what may
Against all odds you kept us true and straight
Your name should be emblazoned, Mary Gray

© All Rights Reserved – 2011 by Lew Gray, Downham Market, Norfolk

ISBN 978-0-9570671-0-3

Printed by
MPG Books Group, Bodmin and King's Lynn

Lew Gray 2011

Contents

Acknowledgement

Here I wish to express my profound gratitude to Elizabeth Blakey for the many hours she has spent deciphering my scrawl and turning it into legible print. Furthermore, I thank her for giving me encouragement when I was thinking about giving up and also for volunteering to deal with any alterations I wished to make, and there were many of them.

Without Elizabeth's support and encouragement this book would never have been published and I shall be eternally grateful.

Lew Gray

Introduction

I was born in the Fenland village of Barroway Drove, where I started my schooling. This was followed by a short amount of time at Wretton school, then back to Barroway Drove until I finished my schooling at Downham Market.

During my formative years my Father was in the Eigth Army (The Desert Rats) all the way through the North Africa Campaign. After that he took part in the invasion of Sicily and Italy where they fought their way up to Monte Casino.

Mother and I lived with Granny and Grandad Napthan at Barroway Drove and Mother worked on the construction, and subsequent maintenance, of R.A.F. Downham Market, where she worked as a bricklayer's labourer and dug trenches by pick and shovel, and mixed concrete by hand. Despite all this hard work, Mother still found the time to teach me to read and write before I started school, for which I have always been truly grateful as it gave me a love of words and books, and I've always thought I was enrolled in The University of Life at a very early age.

So far in this journey of life I have worked in a flour mill, a sugar factory, in agriculture in the black fens around the Methwold/Southery area and in the siltlands and heavy clays of Marshland Fen. In the construction industry I have worked as a bricklayer's labourer, road building, laying kerbstones, paving slabs and pipes, and in civil engineering, building bridges and the construction of large pumphouses for the transference of sewage from one level to another. As for pastimes, I was brought up with guns, ferrets, traps, snares and nets and fishing gear, which was not thought of as a hobby because we only fished for things we could eat, which was mainly for eels, and we also dragged the Tidal Ouse for flatfish. As for sport, I played football and cricket for several local teams and for Station teams while serving with the R.A.F. where my official title was Steward, but I always thought of myself as Refuelling Officer, when serving behind the bar in the Officers' Mess.

Beryl and I were married in 1958 and since then we have had three sons, nine grandchildren, and three great-grandchildren and counting. Having reached the age now when I am no longer capable of performing most of my former pursuits, I have found the time to look back over the years and I find myself amazed at what a mixed bag life has been, for it has also included several visits to various drinking establishments, in which I've always found interesting people, from most walks of life, and a mine of information about the make up of people, most of which is totally useless, although occasionally a gem will emerge from the mix. Although I have always hated beer, I have a bit of a stubborn streak in me, and I'm determined to get used to it, so I keep going back for more.

Having been in so many situations which have triggered so many lines of thought in the making of this mixed bag, I;ve decided to throw a selection of words and thoughts up in the air, in the hope that when they come down again they have landed in some semblance of order. Now they've landed, and the dust has settled, I've decided it's not for me to make any judgement, far better that you form your own opinion and I can only hope you find something to your liking among this selection.

Yours, hopefully

Lew Gray

Norfolk

Golden dawns and crimson sunsets, in a sky both high and wide
Sandbanks, cliffs, and mudflats, ever changing with the tide
Hedgerows, woods and spinneys, an abundance of wild birds
Their song, in such profusion, much too beautiful for words
There are broads, and streams and rivers, and fields of golden
corn
And the heady scent of the hawthorn, complements a mid May
morn
There are cockles, winkles, whelks and crabs, and samphire by
the sea
And if some say we are backward, we'll stay backward willingly

Lew Gray

Comparisons

Although your coat is glossy, and your eyes are bright and clear
Your tail is long, your whiskers neat
You regularly clean your feet
I simply can't afford to have you here

Although you raid my apple store, I really wouldn't mind
If you would only eat the one
But no, you try them all for fun
And leave a trail of havoc there behind

You've eaten all the seed I'd saved, and left me not a scrap
You've chewed my ball of garden string
You've no respect for anything
I'm sorry mouse, but I must set the trap

But wait a bit, have I the right to organise your end
For men will plot and rob for greed
As you did when you stole my seed
And some of them I've thought of as a friend

You're not so very different to humans, I would say
They'll take much more than they can eat
And crush much more beneath their feet
Perhaps I'll set the trap another day

Lew Gray

Appreciations

The cat curled up sleeping in front of the fire
Well groomed and well fed, coat aglow
The dog stirs and whimpers, then settles again
Perhaps dreaming of bones – I don't know.

Beryl watching the telly her feet on a stool
Justin reading, me trying to write
The sweet smell of chestnuts absorbing the heat
Slowly cooking, the fire burning bright.

Wind shrieking, shrilly through telephone wires
Shaking buildings and battering trees
Rain slicing downwards like needles of ice
As the temperature drops by degrees.

There's a changing of seasons, of attitudes too
Winter dampens those yearnings to roam,
The house, taken for granted through warm summer months
Now assumes a new mantle called home

Lew Gray

THE YEARS HAVE FLED

I've always worked to earn a crust, for almost forty years
And in my field, I've always thought, I haven't many peers
I've worked in sun when sweat would run and skin peeled with
the heat
And when the next day came along I'd welcome a repeat

I've worked in snow and ice as well, and fog, and wind, and rain
With fingers cracked and bleeding, quite oblivious to pain
The thing I most appreciate is having had good health
Which any thinking person knows, outweighs all fame or wealth

But gradually the body slows, it's less quick to respond
It struggles to reach places that it used to go beyond
Although I still enjoy my work and do my level best
And still maintain a standard which will withstand any test

I grudge the time it takes me now to earn a living wage
A feeling which is foreign and has grown on me with age
Time is suddenly important now the flush of youth has fled
This time in which I find myself was always years ahead

Too many years have slipped away, I've played them off the cuff
I've worked and played for far too long and never thought enough
There's so much more for me to do, so many things to see
The swifts that scream and play in flight, the busy honey bee

The harvest mice that nest in corn, I once watched as a child
The sunrise of a summer morn, the flowers growing wild
The colours of the rainbow on a stormy afternoon
The afterglow of sunset or a waxing Harvest moon

Apart from this there's family, grandchildren to enjoy
The games they play, the way they laugh, the cunning they em-
ploy
They'll need to go to circuses and play upon the beach
There's shelves to build for ornaments, to keep them out of reach

And so with all these things to do, I think I'll set a date
I hope to have most of it done before I'm ninety eight!

Lew Gray

WORRYING FAREWELL

Striding past the window, just a boy of seventeen
Bulging holdall swinging by his side
Heading for adventure in a search for pastures green
His bonds with home are cut and cast aside

His stride is long and lissom, then he turns to close the gate
He waves farewell, then hurries on his way
His future seems assured to him, for now at any rate
Our youngest son is leaving home today

Born and bred of Norfolk stock, raised in a market town
That sprawls across a hill above the fen
His family of working class, who'd never let you down
Or pander to the whims of other men

How will he cope with problems, which beset him on his way
When there's no one there to turn to for advice
Will he meet with decent people, when he finds a place to stay
Or lay his head where pillows run with lice?

When he's drawn into the cities by the blaze of neon light
Which for any roaming youngster is a must
Will he call to mind the forays in the fenland of a night
When he walked with care to let his eyes adjust

If conmen should approach him, looking for an easy touch
Or if prostitutes should offer him a bed
Or if dealers try to lure him onto heroin and such
Will his country training stand him in good stead?

We have always tried to teach him to distinguish right from
wrong
And to always lend a hand to those in need
And, if possible, to walk away when hard men come along
And to never forfeit quality for speed

We feel we've done our best for him, but now our hands are tied
And the only thing that's left to us is wait
And hope the ship he sails upon, can cope with wind and tide
So that someday he can sail back through our gate

Lew Gray

FIFTY YEARS OF MARRIAGE

It started back in thirty eight, and still it's going strong
Through summers hot and winters cold, and a war that came
along

No elements could stop it, and Hitler did his best
Three children did their level best to amplify the test

Though times were hard and wages low, they never did complain
But worked away in muddy fields, through heat and wind and
rain

They nursed us through our sickness, helped us cope with grow-
ing pains
Chastised us when our clothes were wet from playing in fen
drains

We never did have fancy clothes, we never had the need
But food was always plentiful, some of us verged on greed

They've watched us children grow and leave, to lead our separate
lives
One of us has a husband, and the other two have wives

Grandchildren should have numbered six, but sadly there are five
And Great Grandchildren number three, will any more arrive?

They've reached their Golden Wedding, after having come so far
Tell me, are you interested? do you wonder who they are?

To introduce you to them, makes me feel both proud and glad
To say, meet Lew and Mary Gray, we call them Mum and Dad

So we'd like to bring this message, on this special day for you
We all love and thank you very much, Petula, Jim and Lew

P.S.   Fifty years of wedded bliss, a most impressive score
        So why not raise your sights a bit, and aim for fifty more!

Lew Gray

PERHAPS

Grieve not for me when I am dead
And just my memory remains
But laugh and celebrate instead
For a soul that's free from the body's chains

And think of me on a summer's day
When trees are in full leaf
While witnessing the swifts at play
You'll find no time for grief

Perhaps when I am free to roam
I'll guard the plover's eggs
Or help the honey bees fly home
With pollen laden legs

Perhaps I'll seek a mountain ledge
And visit birds of prey
Or plant a hedge at a desert's edge
And tend it every day

Perhaps I'll join a mountain stream
That chuckles over rocks
Or ply with boats of narrow beam
Negotiating locks

Perhaps I'll help erect a tent
And join a Jamboree
Or mingle with the hawthorn scent
And laze in luxury

Perhaps I'll sail the harvest moon
And revel in its light
Sip nectar from a silver spoon
On each midsummer night

Perhaps I'll make some handles
So to steer a goldfinch charm
Or light some chestnut candles
To illuminate a farm

Perhaps I'll help a blizzard blow
And lay its coat of white
Help children fashion men of snow
You never know, I might

Perhaps I'll gather morning dew
Or revel in the rain
Perhaps if some of this comes true
We'll come to meet again

Lew Gray

Nature's Balance

Daytime hours resting from her efforts of the night
The night used for its cover, not a predator in sight
    Her body subtly merging with the ground on which she lay
    She sleeps, her feet are poised, in case she has to leap away
By afternoon her underside is moist of leaking milk
A warm wind stirs her tawny coat, black flecked and soft as silk
    At dusk, she stirs and stretches, first she has a thirst to slake
    And then she's up and running for she has three calls to make
She lopes along a meadow, keeps a hedgerow on her flank
Passes underneath a gate and pauses near a bank
    She sits up on her haunches, ears erect, detects a sound
    Then homes in on the tiny ball of fur there on the ground
Twin tiny nostrils flaring, slowly dissipating heat
He patiently awaits the dusk and sound of stealthy feet
    His patience is rewarded, as she suddenly appears
    He nuzzles, sucking greedily, she washes round his ears
He finishes his feeding, settles snugly in his form
She finishes the grooming, leaves his coat all moist and warm
    Then she has to leave him, crouching low and on his own
    For she has to feed his sister that he's never even known
The sister hears her coming, and emits an eager cry
The blazing sun has taken toll, and left her parched and dry
    The youngster suckles greedily, soon satisfies her need
    Once groomed, she settles down, aloof, so common of her
breed
The mother, on her way again, stops now and then for food
Then heads towards the third and final member of her brood
    She comes up to the tiny form, in which she thinks he lay
    Not knowing of the drama, which took place there in the day
He lay out in the open, with the cover, brown and sparse

Close to his head, he caught the scent of freshly shooting grass
　　The scent of moisture tempted him, his throat was parched
and dry
　　He moved and broke the golden rule, which meant that he
would die
He'd never even tried the grass he'd seen his mother eat
He reached and snipped a single blade and found it moist and
sweet
　　His appetite was kindled, so he looked around for more
　　Perhaps he wondered why he'd not been shown this grass
before
He was totally committed, his camouflage destroyed
The only chance he had was whether luck was on his side
　　The Peregrine was hunting, be it birds, or rats or mice
　　The small and the unwary would be taken in a trice
She had to make a killing so her youngsters could survive
She saw the movement down below, and went into a dive
　　He saw a fleeting shadow, and stopped as if to check
　　Death came in an instant, as the talons hit his neck
His mother searched for quite a while, called softly once or twice
Eventually, she loped away, she hadn't any choice
　　She had to feed the other two again before the dawn
　　She'd come back here again to search, or would it be to
mourn
The story may seem sad to you, it is, I quite agree
But if she hadn't split them up, she could have lost all three
　　It's all so finely balanced, some must die, so others live
　　And nature seems to judge things, so there's always some to
give.

Lew Gray

21

THE RABBIT LANE LAMENT

Who can convince me that there is a need
To take our allotments away
If you discount unscrupulous, uncaring greed
You'll not find many reasons I'd say

Why must we surrender our last open space
While a few fill their pockets with gold
Should we just knuckle under, just give in with grace
Or should we fight hard to keep hold

What sort of person will put up a hand
To turn bulldozers loose in our town
To rip up our hedges and tear up the land
And to cause our few trees to crash down

Who will deny generations ahead
These few acres where peace can be found
Where crops can be grown, on which mouths can be fed
And the song of wild birds does abound

Where folks can repair with a fork and a hoe
After work, when the day nears its end
With potatoes to plant or with lettuce to sow
And the chance of a chat with a friend

Our allotments are ranged either side of a lane
As are lungs either side of a spine
Twin oases of green, which we hope will remain
Giving air that can taste sweet as wine

Progress is such a convenient word
For those with a fortune to make
But its use in this venture is wholly absurd
And to heed it would be a mistake

I appeal to you planners, please don't let us down
Please don't help the profiteers thrive
This is no dress rehearsal that threatens our town
No, it's curtain up time, and it's LIVE

Lew Gray

THE HUNTER

Just a glint of moonlight silhouettes a willow tree
Whose questing roots draw moisture from the pond
I am waiting for my quarry to present itself to me
Of which, some roam to Russia and beyond.

The waving reeds around me give the cover that I need
As I scan the autumn sky so eagerly
Old Ben waits there beside me with the patience of his breed
His muzzle warm and moist beside my knee

The reeds around us rustle, as the north wind sings its song
And reminds me old man winter is close by
I think about the blizzards that may shortly come along
Then turn my collar up and scan the sky

I think about the Mallard who have fattened on the grain
They have foraged from the stubble fields around
The wheat, the oats, the barley, shaken loose by summer rain
Then scattered by the wind onto the ground

And then I dream of Widgeon, of their eerie haunting call
Of their wheeooing across a winter sky
Of the muzzle flash that halts them like an aircraft in a stall
Of their crashing to the ground, their limbs awry

The dream is interrupted, old Ben gives a warning growl
My muscles tense and flex like supple springs
But then I see what Ben has seen, a silent hunting owl
As it passes overhead on downy wings

Then the duck are with us, just a dozen birds or more
I drop a bird that plummets to the right
But then, before I have a chance of adding to the score
Their frantic wings have taken them from sight

Old Ben takes to the water, to retrieve the fallen duck
He soon returns in triumph with his prize
He showers me with water, then I can't believe my luck
As another group appears before my eyes

They circle my position, then they make their landing run
With wings and paddles set to gather air
Then orange flame is flaring from the barrel of the gun
As death leaps forth to claim the leading pair

The rest veer off in panic, straining hard to gather speed
To take them from this ambush I have laid
The second barrel blossoms and a duck falls in the reed
And Ben sets out agen to ply his trade

A dog fox yaps a message, old Ben gives a throaty growl
As a vixen screams defiance at the night
That chilling, mournful mixture, blending gurgle, moan and how
Uneasily, I pull my jacket tight

The wind picks up a little, and the cloud thins out a bit
The moon looks through a window to the south
Two duck appear, I kill the first, the second is hard hit
Ben soon brings back the first one in his mouth

He turns back to the water, and swims across the pond
I hear him scramble out the other side
He hunts out through the reed bed, then the sedges just beyond
Then brings the drake, his head held high with pride

Now I have sufficient, there's a pair of duck for me
For I didn't come to kill for killing's sake
The family next door is large, so they can do with three
And old Annie down the lane shall have the drake

I am at an early breakfast, the clock shows ten to three
I am planning to be out to see the dawn
My trusty gun, and faithful dog, will not be there with me
So I feel a trifle saddened and forlorn

The gun is oiled and locked away, it's been that way for years
Old Ben lies in the garden, buried deep
At times my eyes will moisten, and I'm close to shedding tears
For Bed still walks beside me when I sleep

The bag I take down from the wall has been a constant friend
But its lining still bears stains of ancient blood
Of Mallard, Teal and Widgeon, who have come to meet their end
As I've taken full advantage of the flood

The bag could tell of broken wings, of plumage seeping blood
Of trips through muddy creeks close by the sea
Of Pintail and of Gadwall, who have crashed down in the mud
And of Goldeneye, with eyes that could not see

Then suddenly I realise, I'm looking back again
And the only way to look is look ahead
For memories, however fond, will also bring some pain
So I'll look toward the living, not the dead

A video recorder will be in the bag today
With binocular and sandwiches as well
As I'm hunting down my my quarry, in a very different way
So the bag will have a better tale to tell

Lew Gray

PROGRESS

Acres of rooftops with roads in between
Patios paved, so no earth can be seen
Driveways of concrete with neat rounded edge
Fences of brickwork, no sign of a hedge

Playgrounds of tarmac in which children run
Raceways of asphalt hold cars built for fun
Motorway miles, crushing all underneath
Be it hillside, or valley, or bogland or heath

Together they form an impervious cloak
So the rain from the skies has nowhere to soak
The earth underneath is both sterile and sad
Locked so firmly away from the allies it had

Its allies, the sun and the wind and the rain
Would it know them should ever it meet them again
For the wind once so fresh, is now poisoned by sprays
The rain laced with acid, that eats and decays

The layer of ozone is riddled with holes
Caused by gasses from cans which are called aerosols
The sun, now unfiltered, is melting the Poles
How long will it be 'til the Lutine Bell tolls?

But we press on regardless, and stick to our tasks
With our thick rubber gloves and our health saving masks
For we haven't an option, no safe place to go
One word describes all, it's called progress you know

Lew Gray

28

ENGLISH YEAR

How will I capture a mid May morn
When the heady scent of the hawthorn's bloom
Enriches air, on which are borne the silken
Threads from a spider's loom

I hear the scream of the swifts at play
And the cuckoos call from a nearby tree
And I wish, if only time could stay
And May would reign eternally

I stop, aghast, what would I do?
Condemn forever, June's delights
For should my selfish wish come true
There'd be no more midsummer nights

To wish to miss a July dawn
When every tree is in full leaf
Or miss the bloom on turning corn
Is lunacy beyond belief

And what of August, laced with sun
When fishes rise from quiet pools
When holidaying kids have fun
And farmers look to harvest tools

September's quiet, balmy days
Bring scents of lush, maturing fruit
And wasps embark on food forays
And schoolboys quickly follow suit

Big brother to the gentle breeze
We've come to know these recent weeks
Increases speed and batters trees
I smile and know October speaks

A starry night, a frost at dawn
Which flees before the rising sun
Leaves turn to copper, brown and fawn
Which means November has begun

The leaves have fallen, trees are bare
The land enjoys a well earned rest
December, Christmas, time to share
And children act their very best

A brand new year, the frost is hard
Long nights, log fires and winter's tales
Now sea defences double guard
Awaiting January's gales

Soon days grow longer, blizzards blow
As February dons its dress
And children fashion men of snow
Below, plants stir in readiness

In readiness because they know
That spring is not too far away
Though snow may fly when March winds blow
Their colours will shine bright and gay

Now martins drift across the sky
And swallows soon will follow on
'Midst April showers blossoms fly
Amazingly a year has gone

And so, it's time to summarise
I've quickly scanned an English year
In doing so I realise
That every month holds something dear

I feel I must withdraw my plea
That May alone should reign supreme
Far better that the year run free
With quiet moments left to dream

Lew Gray

The Demise of the Songthrush

There's an obsolete anvil out there in my yard
And its silence is worrying me
It's both pretty and ugly, dull, shiny and hard
And there's lots of soft colours to see

It must have spent aeons of time in the dark
As it travelled a glacier's way
It probably introduced man to the spark
And it's still serving man to this day

But of late it's been spending its time in the light
And providing a service as well
To the songthrush who find its rough surface just right
When they're breaking a snail from its shell

Time was, when I'd wake with the breaking of dawn
With the dawn chorus well under way
And the blackbirds already at work on the lawn
As they sought their first meal of the day

Or I'd wake to the sound of shell upon stone
As a thrush broke a shell from a snail
It would patiently work, like a dog with a bone
And they'd win in the end, without fail

Or they'd search through the lilies that grow by the hedge
Where the snails try to hide through the day
Or they'd hunt through the stones at the rockery's edge
Or perhaps find a fat slug to slay

I still wake with the dawn, as a countryman will
The dawn chorus still pleases my ear
The blackbirds are seemingly getting their fill
But the thrushes are absent, I fear

There are no heaps of shells at the foot of the stone
No thrush sings its song from a tree
And I'm certain it stems from one reason alone
I'll explain it, perhaps you'll agree

There are pellets produced to kill both slug and snail
Which are strewn by the gardener's hand
And the farmers distribute each year without fail
And I'm certain that this should be banned

So the pellets are strewn, then the snail comes along
To feed, as they do, through the night
It will feed on the pellets, which prove its swan song
And it fails to get back out of sight

It will die on the footpath, with more of its kind
Who had fed on the pellets as well
Each one leaving unusual trails there behind
As froth oozes out from its shell

At daybreak a songthrush arrives at the scene
To find breakfast served, as on a plate
It will breakfast on snails and leave the plates clean
And unwittingly hasten its fate

With its appetite sated, the thrush flies away
To bathe, and to preen, and to rest
But the poison will work by the end of the day
And its young ones will die in their nest

If a pet dog is poisoned, or maybe a cat
You would all get upset and cry 'shame'
But what of the songthrush, just think about that
Why don't you react just the same

Lew Gray

Our Dad

His life was never easy, but he rose above it all
He'd work away in sun, or wind, or rain
Stood stalwart, as our anchor, picked us up if we should fall
Ot would comfort us if we should suffer pain

His first love was his family, he loved us one and all
He would always be around to give advice
And would listen to our problems, were they big or were they
small
Sometimes he'd frown and say 'that isn't nice'

He loved the fields and hedgerows, and he loved the woodland
glade
He'd greet each stream and river as a friend
He loved a bit of fishing, 'neath the willows, in the shade
And loved a yard of healthy stock to tend

He loved a game of cricket, when in bat he'd chance his luck
He played it as it should be, as a game
And if the scorer had to write, Lew Gray, out for a duck
He'd laugh and say 'Len Hutton's done the same'

He would search along the hedgerows, or hunt the woodland
through
For sticks, from which he'd make a walking aid
Of holly, blackthorn, alder, nut, to name but just a few
To him it was a pleasure, not a trade

One thing he really hated, yes, he really hated war
He hated it for all the lives it claimed
The fact he'd lost six years of youth, hurt like an open sore
He came back home, both shell and bullet maimed

He has fought his final battle, it was one he couldn't win
And soon we'll place his body 'neath the sod
He didn't want to leave us, and he never did give in
And seemed to find the strength to wrestle God

For now, we're left with memories, of which we're truly fond
And he can rest in peace, and free from pain
As he travels on his journey out into the great beyond
Someday, pray God, we'll come to meet again

Lew Gray

Sleepless Nights

Hopeless faces, empty pockets and despair
Mortgage payments, glaring overdue
An ageing car, in dire need of repair
Decisions made three years ago to rue

Decisions which were never lightly made
They borrowed what their income would allow
When moneylenders came to ply their trade
Things looked so very different from now

Come, borrow, no repayment 'til next year
Good advertising led them to the web
Their salaries suffice, so nought to fear
Then suddenly the tide began to ebb

The company they worked for did them proud
Its order books were bursting at the seams
Then it suddenly lay dead beneath a shroud
And nightmares quickly took the place of dreams

Since rates of interest have doubled up
And Poll Tax costs are twice as much as rates
They realise they've drawn a bitter cup
The victim of a trap with cunning baits

At first they seemed to manage fairly well
With money from redundancy to spend
But now it's gone, and worry casts its spell
Sad days and sleepless nights, where will it end?

Lew Gray

Summer Day

Night-time creatures slowing
Dawning of the day
Distant cockerel crowing
Scent of curing hay

Hipshot horses stamping
Rising summer sun
Boy Scouts summer camping
Tents let down in fun

Meadow grasses blowing
Poppyheads ablaze
Pure spring water flowing
Shimmering heat haze

Length of shadows growing
Red sun dips away
Sound of cattle lowing
Closing of the day

Lew Gray

A Day Out

We were off work on Friday, both Beryl and me
We drove out to the country, the blossom to see
There were Horse Chestnut candles, of pale creamy white
And occasional red ones to add to delight

The fragrance of Hawthorn, the locals call May
The Cow Parsley waves as we go on our way
Shadowy archways a mixture of green
Pale sunlight filters its way through the screen

Magnificent Beech, massive trunks glowing grey
The leaves whisper to us this warm summer day
Massed Rhododendrons ablaze 'neath the trees
The call of the Cuckoo drifts in on the breeze

Now all this is behind us, we are nearing the coast
With its tang of salt breezes, and lunch, a nice roast

Lew Gray

Sad Facts

The pale shrunken face is now looking serene
As though dreaming again of what just might have been
The thin wasted body lies under the shroud
Just a shadow of what was once robust and proud

Abandoned by children, her husband long dead
Too much trouble for those she kept clothed and fed
They'll return here to see her placed under the sod
Let us pray she receives better treatment from God

Lew Gray

THE DARKEST SUNNY DAY

I watched the procession in deep despair
    and I longed to hear her say
I am Diana, the Queen of Hearts
    and I am here to stay

But the horses walked at a steady pace
    and the people lined the road
Six horses pulled a carriage
    with, oh, such a heavy load

The carriage bore a Nation's grief
    and tears flowed past its wheels
The pace was slow, and now I know,
    how a daytime nightmare feels

I prayed someone would wake me up
    and say, 'It's all a dream'
But the horses stepped, and the people wept
    and I screamed a silent scream

But the horses stepped, and the people wept
    her children followed proud
Their feelings numb, as they mourned their mum
    asleep beneath the shroud

The horses stepped, and the people wept
    the Nation held its breath
As it longed relief from the aching grief
    borne by this thief called Death

The horses stepped a steady pace
　　but soon their steps would cease
Their job well done, her race well run
　　Pray God she'll rest in peace

I'll remember her for her loving care
　　for her nervous flashing eyes
For her quiet restraint, was she a saint
　　in beautiful disguise?

Lew Gray

The Meadow

Close to us lay a meadow, untended by man
I shall duly describe it to you if I can
It was not of a level, it sloped to the West
And nature ensured it was charmingly dressed

It was bounded by hedges of hawthorn and rose
Which were planted as shelter for stock, I suppose
In the top northern corner some springs bubbled up
And marsh marigold grew, which we knew as Kingcup

The springs ran together and formed a small rill
Which slowly meandered its way down the hill
It skirted small hillocks and bunches of sedge
Yellow Flag water iris grew there at its edge

Children would come and would sail their small ships
Fashion chains out of daisies or gather cowslips
Or they'd play hide and seek and their laughter would ring
Or fire arrows from bows made of willow and string

They would find sticks and stones and small tussocks of grass
Then assemble a dam, so no water could pass
Then they'd eagerly wait for the water to rise
When the dam broke, some cheered others squealed mock surprise

The rill fed the pond at the end of the field
Which the children all loved for the things it could yield
The seasons dictated which items they'd bring
Sometimes they'd bring jam jars with handles of string

Or they'd bring willow rods and their home made cork floats
And packed lunches made bulges in pockets of coats
They would gather the frogspawn, swap minnows for newts
Capture stag water beetles, ply other pursuits

Then they'd eat their packed lunches, with never a thought
For hands covered in slime from the eels they had caught
Before sunset, adventure would end for the day
They would gather their spoils and would go on their way

Taking home the tall reedmace or pink dogrose bud
To mollify mothers, their clothes caked with mud
The autumn brought fruits from the things growing wild
Which were sought out by all, from grandparent to child

Crab apples were gathered for jelly to make
Sometimes eaten by children, whose stomachs would ache
Hazel nuts were a prize, and were picked in a trice
There was much competition from squirrels and mice

Lawyers' wigs would be gathered, so slender and round
Horse mushrooms and puffballs grew close on the ground
Walking sticks were employed to pull blackberries down
And a brush with a bramble caused many a frown

Mulberries were picked, leaving hands in a mess
The stream would be waded to pick watercress
Sloes curled the tongue, causing faces to grin
But were gathered by many for making sloe gin

There was so much to do, there was so much at stake
We just took it for granted, we made a mistake
The old lady who'd owned the small meadow for years
Then died, and was buried, the town shed its tears

She had but one relation, a nephew they say
He came to the town, never meaning to stay
He had been left a house, the small meadow as well
He just wanted the money, and came here to sell

The house went on the market and sold straight away
The meadow was auctioned, it proved a sad day
For the peace of the meadow would cease in a flash
When a man came along with unlimited cash

Several locals made bids, but they all proved in vain
For the man with the cash bid again and again
They just couldn't match him, whatever they did
When the hammer came down, he had made the last bid

His chatter was smooth, his appearance élan
When he went to the council to forward a plan
He convinced them the town needed someone like him
How the whole town would profit and pockets would brim

So his plan was accepted, then contractors came
But within the first week all the people cried, shame
The stream was diverted, the hedgerows were raped
The contours of the meadow were torn and reshaped

Wildlife was scattered, some crushed by machines
Men sweated and swore, in their mud spattered jeans
For a few days the Lapwings flew over, bemused
Nevermore would their ancestral nest sites be used

Neither would Snipe leap to fast jinking flight
Or the Nightingales sing in the still of the night
The Kingfisher was robbed of his old fishing place
He would now have to find other waters to grace

For the pond was filled in and the fish had all died
Children watched through the chainlink and most of them cried
For the old folk, the fruits of wild harvest were lost
Now they sit in their houses, no doubt counting cost

The cost of the jams, the fruit for a pie
The nuts of the Hazel, or mushrooms to fry
In place of the meadow a corn store now stands
The whole business is run by just two pairs of hands

Now the children walk streets, some have turned into yobs
What a hideous price we have paid for two jobs
Our meadow was one, there are so many more
Perhaps you are blessed and have one by your door

If you have, and it's threatened, then fight tooth and nail
You children should cry, and you women should wail
And you men, stir yourselves, go and rattle doorknobs
Don't be conned by the promise of mythical jobs

For even the smallest of towns needs a place
For the wildlife to live, for the slowing of pace
Giving peace to the old, and adventure to young
By daylight a picture, by night, a third lung

Lew Gray

That Year

That year was most yewnewsual, though I can't recall the date
Good Friday was in August, and Christmas day was late

The rain poured down for weeks on end, but ponds and streams were dry
Frogs moved at the gallop, but we never found out why

Free range hens all went on strike, so cockerels laid the eggs
Dogs ignored the lampposts, and refused to lift their legs

Rainbows weren't bowed that year, each one was ruler straight
Cat hurling was abolished from our local garden fete

The sun would rise at midnight, and the moon was always full
And a filly who was silly, lost her honour to a bull

Snow was used as stuffing, and boiled eggs turned out fried
Crows got caught in spiders' webs, and many of them died

Apple trees had plums on, and the runner beans just walked
Action groups just wouldn't act, they simply sat and talked

Dogs gave birth to kittens, and pork resembled beef
Hay took the place of poultry, and the poultry sighed relief

Cats gave birth to puppies, and the Billygoats behaved
Rhubarb caused constipation, and Father Christmas shaved

Hedgehogs wore their spines inside, and badgers were all red
They had swapped their coats with foxes who were black and
white instead

Ducks and geese refused to swim, pigs took to the skies
My mother had a son that year, and he tells bloody lies

Lew Gray

Some Adventures Of The Town Clock

It started as a wristwatch, so I've heard old people say
   But with time it's grown in stature into what it is today
It has stood on guard for ages, facing north, south, east and west
   And though it's not been perfect, I am sure it's done its best
It has known all kinds of weather, such as blizzards, wind and rain
   But it stands on sound foundations which can withstand any strain
It has witnessed many changes, some for better, some for worse
   And some I find too difficult to organise in verse
It once had two companions to converse with through the night
   But someone moved the old town pump and placed it out of sight
The other, the pagoda (which had many tales to tell)
   Dealt quietly with people's needs and gave relief as well
The pagoda was demolished, some folks rubbed their hands with glee
   Perhaps the town hall will survive, we'll have to wait and see
Perhaps the clock feels lonely now the market stalls have gone
   And with them all the market cries of Billy, Ruth and John
No more will people mingle, searching, buying this and that
   Perhaps meet up with dear old friends and stop to have a chat
Just recently the clock stood fast as scenes of chaos reigned
   As streets and pavements were destroyed (Thank God, it hardly rained)
It found itself surrounded by JCBs and trucks
   An oasis was created as a home for plastic ducks
Paving slabs and kerbs were laid, and most of them looked nice
   But then they took them up again and laid most of the twice

50

They built a new pagoda, then they found the site was wrong

Perhaps they should have fitted wheels to help it move along

But finally the job was done, relief came to the town

The clock surveyed the scene, and I am sure it wore a frown

Perhaps it felt neglected, it was certainly ignored

Eventually a cry was heard 'THE CLOCK WILL BE RE-STORED'

They surrounded it with scaffolding bedecked with plastic sheets

And so the clock was blinded and could not survey the streets

Men worked inside the cladding 'til the clock was clean and bright

Then gave it many coats of paint of black and green and white

Other men worked deep inside, which wasn't very nice

And restored its vital organs, so to give it back its voice

Eventually the job was done, the scaffold taken down

And so the clock could see again and keep watch on the town

The council held a meeting and decided on a time

To switch it on officially, so folks could hear it chime

Folks assembled in their droves, and children held balloons

But then a scene unfolded like an excerpt from The Goons

For when they needed access to a lever placed inside

They couldn't open up the door, no matter how they tried

I'm sure the clock turned awkward, and it wouldn't let them in

Had anyone looked up, they might have seen a four-faced grin

Eventually it opened, but they didn't turn it on

It wouldn't chime again 'til five, with four o'clock long gone

I'm sure the old clock chortled – did it rub its hands with glee?

For when they turned it on at five, it just chimed ONE, TWO, THREE

51

Some folks found it amusing while they smiled, some wore a
frown
 Some said it was the best show since the cinema closed down
Now we've half an amphitheatre, was it once a part of Rome?
 Whatever, I am certain we'll make it feel at home
And so, to make it welcome and to make the job complete
 Perhaps we should race chariots around our one-way street

Lew Gray
September 2004

Wat-er Waste

I come from haunts of Coot and Herne, Lord Tennyson once
wrote
When water ran to river, stream, or dyke, or pond or moat

He wrote about a stream which said that man may come and go
While it, the stream, would eddy, surge but never cease to flow

It could not have had an inkling what the future held in store
Or it wouldn't have been certain it would flow for evermore

Technology has aided those who live and thrive on greed
To organise a system, to commit their darkest deed

They sink their pipes deep in the earth to caverns deep and dark
A practice which is common to the modern day landshark

They draw up precious water, which is hurled up to the skies
Of which most will evaporate before your very eyes

Though some of it will help the crop and give a better yield
As plastic pipes are moved in turn to each potato field

But some are still not satisfied, and plant a second crop
Create a glut, then whine and moan when prices start to drop

This second crop is planted when the land is warm and dry
Which means more precious water is hurled up to the sky

Where most of it is wasted , as it meets with wind and sun
And common sense should tell us, it is being overdone

This cannot go on for ever, better methods must be found
There's a limit to this water, once stored safely underground

It's the middle of winter, we have had torrential rain
There is nothing on the surface, it has disappeared again

Rushing down to those deep caverns which are raided year on
year
Would Lewis Carroll's Carpenter have shed a bitter tear?

Our wetlands are receding, and some river beds are dry
It does not need an expert to explain the reason why

They are squandering the staff of life on which we all depend
If no one will apply the brake, I see a dismal end

We must have irrigation, so the scientists all say
But we must control our water in a more efficient way

We must ensure our rivers thrive, our springs and streams must
flow
So come on you technologists, you've quite a way to go

Lew Gray

Motorway Madness

Motorway morons, dual carriageway fools
    Sit smug at the wheels of their murdering tools
On B roads and by roads they act just the same
    As they practice their skills at the lunacy game
It seems such a pity we cannot afford
    To build special roads, just for those who are bored
Who cannot wait a second, and must overtake
    Irrespective of how many lives are at stake
They could all get together, each practice their skill
    And each one could find fellow loonies to kill
But the carnage goes on, doesn't anyone care
    Of the girl from next door, with the beautiful hair
Or the boy down the street with mischievous eyes
    They were buried today amidst weeping and sighs
Each morning someone will leave home with a wave
    And a few miles away be condemned to the grave
Condemned to the grave by one who was late
    And put throttle to floor, as he shot out the gate
And continued to drive, like a bat out of hell
    'Til a rending of metal, a scream and a yell
Means bones have been broken, and blood has been spilled
    As a sensible breadwinning parent is killed
But was it the fault of the man who was late
    And put throttle to floor, as he shot out the gate?
Oh no, not a bit, he was fully in charge
    As he threatened the lives of the public at large
Nor could he be blamed for the bend in the road
    Or the slow moving vehicle, with extra wide load
That caused him to swerve to the opposite side
    In the path of a car in which somebody died

Well that's what he said, when a crowd gathered round
    To tend to the body, which lay on the ground
What will he be fined, if he's taken to court?
    It's amazing how cheaply a life can be bought
He'll be fined, but a pittance, for taking the life
    Of a man with two daughters, a son and a wife
And walk free from the court, treat the verdict with scorn
    While a widow, a son and two daughters still mourn
We need a deterrent, to start saving lives
    To weed out the loonies, whose action deprives
Children of fathers, or husbands of wives
    But we still allow luck to decide who survives
Here's a message for those who treat driving as fun
    When you drive, put your car on a par with a gun
They can be just as lethal, so drive them with care
    And remember the girl with the beautiful hair
And remember the children in hospital beds
    Their tiny limbs mangled, and plates in their heads
Poor innocent victims, who lie there and moan
    Perhaps crippled for life through no fault of their own
Some of these have a parent to blame for their plight
    Due to driving too fast on a dark, foggy night
But most can blame strangers for laying them low
    One who wasn't quite sure, but decided to go
And pulled out of the traffic approaching a curve
    Met an oncoming vehicle and caused it to swerve
And career off the road, turning end over end
    All because of a stranger who passed on a bend
And what of the stranger, he drove on of course
    But what did he feel, was it guilt or remorse?

Whe would hazard a guess, at the thoughts of this kind
    Who just bulldoze along and leave carnage behind
Could it be they have keys of the twin action kind
    Which can switch on the engine, and switch off the mind
There will always be youngsters who think that it's great
    To put throttle to floor, and career through the gate
Some will corner too fast and end up in a fence
    And you'd think the survivors would learn common sense
But, alas, there are many who reach middle age
    And continue to drive as though seething with rage
There must be a reason for action like this
    Could it be, a car door represents an abyss
And that once they're inside, they step out into space
    To become mindless monsters involved in a race
Or is it aggression that comes to the fore
    Or perhaps they feel safe at the click of a door
Perhaps deep emotions they've kept locked away
    Crack through the veneer and are brought into play
To intimidate all who would dare cross their path
    So they'd either back off, or would risk a bloodbath
Although long winded speeches are not in my style
    If my thoughts save one life, it has all been worthwhile

Lew Gray

Resilient Oak

A century has slipped away since this, once mighty, oak
Threw shadow of a summer's day, dressed in its leafy cloak

It dwarfed all opposition, overshadowed them by far
From its slightly raised position on the gently sloping carr

Its massive trunk was gnarled and tough, its widespread limbs
were strong
Its surface roots were wiry, and its taproot thick and long

It stood for near three hundred years, withstanding every test
But then another tree crashed down, a half a mile to West

The tree that fell produced the seed, from which this one had
grown
And when it fell, it blocked a stream, and seeds of death were
sown

The tree that blocked the stream had stood five hundred years and
more
Until a bolt of lightening struck, and split it to the core

The stream brought debris with it, which entangled with the tree
A dam was formed, held water back which previously ran free

The water level lifted, and it spread across the land
'Til it found a long depression, where the wind had scoured the
sand

At first it merely trickled, filled each crevice it could find
Then its speed increased, as pressure slowly built up from behind

The water travelled onwards, skirting clumps of sedge and gorse
And the small depression deepened, and the stream had changed
its course

It ran along excitedly, surveyed its new domain
Paused now and then, 'til reinforcements pushed it on again

The oak which stood three hundred years, stood dominant, su-
preme
Its greedy roots drank water from the redirected stream

This all happened in late summer, the water levels low
But autumn came, with days of rain, and water had to flow

The upland shrugged its shoulders, shedding water like a cloak
The water had no choice, but find some other land to soak

But soaking was not good enough, the rain did not abate
The waters rushed to join the stream, which soon ran in full spate

The tranquil stream of summer disappeared before its wrath
And it stripped all vegetation which was lying in its path

With soil exposed, the water cut the gently sloping banks
And tiny upright cliffs stood up, in undulating ranks

The water undercut the cliffs, which fell, to wash away
And so the stream grew wider, and it came to pass this way

The banks were built of layers, alternating sand and peat
And this oak of three hundred years, felt water at its feet

The stream grew ever wider, and a mass of roots lay bare
Like crooked fingers, searching for succour that was not there

Its surface roots washed clean of soil, the tree swayed in the
breeze
Its taproot like the thread that held the sword of Damocles

Its leaves soon lost their glossiness, for which they were re-
nowned
The wind increased, the taproot snapped, the tree crashed to the
ground

Small branches snapped like rifle shots, and massive limbs were
rent
All vegetation in its path was broken, torn or bent

The wind sang on regardless, but all wildlife held its breath
Perhaps it paused to mourn this mighty tree's untimely death

Time passed, and nature dressed the wound inflicted on the
ground
As each plant found its habitat, of hollow, niche or mound

A mass invasion soon took place, as hordes of insects came
To bore or burrow, cut or chew, each species laid its claim

60

Some of them burrowed shallowly, just underneath the bark
While other types, with other needs, bored tunnels deep and dark

Soon many types of fungi came, each species found its slot
Invading cracks and crevices, its presence causing rot

Rabbits burrowed 'neath the trunk, and scattered earth around
A grave was slowly fashioned and the tree sank in the ground

This giant which once graced the sky, erect, aloof and proud
Lies at my feet, recumbent, 'neath a moss and lichen shroud

The stream no longer comes this way, it's changed its course
again
The tree that formed the dam broke up, though fragment still
remain

Why did it come here anyway? I stand and wonder, why
Should nature choose to kill this tree, then leave it high and dry

Perhaps it's part of nature's plan, where some things have to give
Their very lives, in order that some other species live

Although it lost its link with life, a hundred years ago
And its merging with the earth has been insidiously slow

It's given home and shelter to so many different things
Assisting nature in her ways, of roundabouts and swings

An acorn which this tree produced, is growing here, close by
This youngster, of two hundred years, now dominates the sky

And it, in turn, has thrown its seed, a few of which have grown
And they, in turn, no doubt will soon grow acorns of their own

Its toughness and resilience should bode well for its clan
Provided it can find a way to cope with ways of man

Lew Gray

A Need to Eat, a Need to Kill

Those years ago, when we were poor
    And hunger knocked at every door
We'd pit our wits with traps and snares
    To catch the wild things unawares
'Most everything we caught we'd eat
    A sparrow pie went down a treat
Blackbirds, Pigeons, Moorhens too
    Would make a very tasty stew
Sometimes we'd really be in luck
    And catch a rabbit, or a duck
At times like this, we'd feel replete
    With such delicious food to eat
I don't feel proud of what I did
    When I was just a hungry kid
But hunger can drive anyone
    To trap, or snare, or use a gun
Now times have changed, so no one needs
    To practice these uncaring deeds
Though some will always ply their skill
    To satisfy their need to kill
That need which seems to deflagrate
    Is, sadly, just a human trait

Lew Gray

Eric Golding and Barroway Drove CC
50 not out

The club was formed in forty eight, and still it's going strong
As older men hung up their boots, so youngsters came along

The Club would never have been formed, well that's what I suppose
But for the generosity of Mr Harold Rose

He said the Club could use his field, and laid a concrete wicket
The Club then bought a mat and gear, and started playing cricket

To get into the field, we walked a plank across a dyke
I'll bet those folk who play at Lords have never seen the like

Dress was very casual, no two players dressed the same
But weren't judged on how they looked, but how they played the game

Some people played in overalls, and some in pin striped suits
And a fellow from Rings End turned up to play in football boots

We hadn't any gear to spare, both pads and gloves were sparse
And balls were at a premium, they got lorst in long grass

The ladies were supportive, they'd come, pushbikes laden down
With cups and plates and sandwiches, they'd never let us down

But we hadn't a pavilion or electricity
So they always brought a primus, to heat water for the tea

They just had a trestle table, and no matter what the weather
When an innings ended they'd say 'come yew on tergether'

They'd give us cakes, and sandwiches, of cheese, or potted meat
To be washed down with cups of tea, and we'd soon feel replete

Those concrete wickets caused some pain, if you were bowling fast
I found the biggest problem was to get some boots to last

And I know what I'm saying, for I have a legacy
Its in between my ankle and my hip, a knackered knee
You talk about all rounders, well we must have had the best
The things we had to play round would put anyone to test

We had to play round mole hills, cowpats, nettles, docks
And that worn't a bit unusual to get thistles in your socks

Most of the fields were much the same, one instance I recall
Was when John Venni dived and tried to catch a speeding ball

He failed, but had he caught it, what a catch it would have been
But he slithered through a cowpat and his clothes were turned to green

The batsman had been lucky, all his runs came of the edge
He edged them through and over slips, some wound up in the hedge

Johny strolled up to him, and the batsman's pride was hurt
When Johny said 'You've had more shit than I've got on my
shirt'

One day at Walpole Highway, Neville Griffin made us stare
When he sped toward the boundary, like a thick set Fred Astaire

But Nev was over eager, and we'd never seen the like
When he did a pirouette and disappeared into a dyke

The dyke was full of bottles, tins, and prams and bikes and all
David Fendley shouted 'Leave all that, just find the bloody ball'

The language from the dyke was foul, I won't say what was said
But the ladies making tea were shocked, some of them turned
quite red

Some players used to turn up drunk, and many people say
It started when John Cox arrived and led the lads astray

And do you know, they could be right, for when I stop and think
Until I first met up with John I'd never had a drink

Cyril Griffin played one day, when we were short of men
But after that experience, he didn't play agen

He went to throw the ball in, but it flew the other way
And so forty grazing cattle then decided they would play

With tails erect they rushed about, and some began to bawl
The batsman ran eleven runs, then someone called, 'lorst ball'

Cyril went among the cattle, and they charged him left and right
He shouted 'I just want the ball, I didn't come here to fight'

And later, as he left the field, he said 'I don't like cricket
Oh no, it's far too dangerous, in future you can stick it'

Terry Good kept wicket, and he loved to swing a bat
And one day at the Metal Box, he certainly did that

He hit one to the factory, It disappeared within
The ball was never found, perhaps it wound up in a tin

When I think of wicketkeepers, Chick Lewis springs to mind
He stood four square behind the stumps, like others of his kind

When we were just a pair of lads, that's me and Adrian Height,
Chick said 'Now listen here, you boys, and I shall put you right'

'When you throw the ball in, you must throw it at my head
Then I'll have to catch it, otherwise I'll end up dead"

About ten minutes later, the ball came out to me
I picked it up and hurled it back, perhaps too hurriedly

The ball sped in toward the stumps, I really let it go
But then, alas, the ball hit Chick on top of his big toe

But Chick was wearing plimsolls, so his face looked pained and red
When he shouted 'You young hellion, I'm not standing on my head'

Another wicket keeper was adept, alert and spry
And when Springheels stood behind the stumps, there never was
a bye

When he was in position, we would never need a slip
He'd spring and leap, and roll and dive, he had a vice-like grip

He worried many batsmen, and they still relate the tales
Of how they strayed a half an inch, and he whipped off the bails

One who shall be nameless, told us all one Saturday
I feel I'm really in top form, I'll show them how to play

He quickly got his eye in, and the runs began to flow
But when he got to thirty, he received a body blow

He crawled to the pavilion, where he squirmed inside his socks
His Mrs said 'You silly fool, you should have worn a box'

We played a match one evening, or at least we started to
But their umpire started cheating, and that caused a right old do

Nev Griffin strode out to the crease, but didn't take a bat
He pulled up all the metal pegs, and then rolled up the mat

He told them 'Pack your bags and go, we've seen enough of you
And do us all a favour, take your cheating umpire too'

Four of us would struggle with that mat, well normally
But Nev was so fired up that night, he spurned the other three

He braced his heavy shoulders, and then picked up the mat
He hurled it in the storeroom, then grinned and said 'Howzat?'

Another umpire I recall, he wasn't one of ours
He didn't only count the balls, he'd also count the hours

If you opened up the innings, or you batted number eleven
Then you'd be out, and he'd be in, the pub at dead on seven

A visitor strode to the crease, took guard, then took his stance
We noticed there was something wrong with but a single glance

The single pad he wore was on the leg behind the crease
I looked at him and thought, my word, will wonders never cease

When someone told him it was wrong, he said 'I know my friend
But that'll be alright when I get up that other end"

My father played, I played myself, and so did both my sons
Who knows, perhaps my grandson will soon get amongst the runs

My father would have loved this day, but died a year ago
His bowling arm was very good, his batting wasn't so

He's gone the way of Harry Bell, Bill Crofts and Terry Rye
Let's hope they're playing cricket on some pitch up in the sky

I've mentioned several names today, and no doubt missed a few
Not because you're not important, for without the likes of you

The club would not have flourished, no it would have gone the way
Of many other clubs we knew, that don't exist today

So now, down to the reason we are gathered here today
It's to celebrate with Eric, for his fifty years of play

Well fifty cricket seasons, is a most impressive score
So Eric, raise your sights a bit, and aim for fifty more

Lew Gray - 1998

Teamwork

My boys and me made a thousand runs last Sunday afternoon
Justin made sixty four not out which proved to be a boon
Stuart weighed in with thirty six, which made the century
So the duck I scored tagged on the end, made the thousand up
you see

Lew Gray - July 1998

Reflections

I love those nights both cold and dark
When Tawnys hoot and Barn owls scream
When trees stand leafless, bare and stark
I walk alone, feel free to dream
To dream of days of lesser pace
When people had more time to muse
Before world leaders formed a race
To build an atom bomb to fuse

Of days when I was just a boy
When cattle stood knee deep in straw
Before the village shop, our joy
Succumbed to supermarkets' maw
When hoes were wielded in the fields
And sprays were hardly ever used
To murder weeds and boost crop yields
The poison makers stand accused

The countryside was quieter then
When man and horse worked side by side
Through farmyards roamed the free range hen
And people did their work with pride
We'd search through barns, and sheds, and ricks
For wayward hens who wished to brood
They'd soon emerge with tender chicks
And teach them how to scratch for food

Large wagons pulled by heavy shires
And decked with raves for larger loads
And massive wheels with iron tyres
Crushed stones along the metalled roads
The harvest times seemed warm and long
Men worked and sweated in the heat
The skylark sang its rippling song
And rabbits fled on flying feet

Cow parsley grew beside the road
Where yellowhammers loved to nest
Turned stones revealed a resting toad
And ponds held newts with upraised crests
Wildflowers used to please the eye
With colours now so rarely seen
Since herbicides caused them to die
We're left with sickly shades of green

Both men and women worked the land
And friendly banter used to flow
Tall cornstacks stood, erect and grand
In silhouette at afterglow
The English partridge graced the land
And laid its eggs by hedge or dyke
You'd count them now upon one hand
Whoever thought we'd see the like

The traction engines came to farms
Their workmates followed, line astern
And farmers stood with open arms
'Midst water carts with coal to burn
To walk here offers some escape
From pressures progress brought along
From news of murder, greed and rape
But not, alas, for very long

Have standards dropped so very low
A race once proud, become uncouth
Or is it me that thinks it so
Through pique at loss of treasured youth

Lew Gray

Full Circle

Have you ever stopped to think
    When pouring liquid down the sink
Where does it go, what does it do
    When out of sight of me and you
What chemicals does it contain
    As it goes rushing down the drain
We love to see our sinks shine bright
    But if you thought, you might take fright
There's liquids just for washing up
    Each knife, each fork, each plate, each cup
There's pads to scrub the saucepans clean
    And what does biologic mean
They say it gobbles up the dirt
    To give your child the whitest shirt
There's washing powder, toilet soap
    Some of which comes on a rope
The disinfectant smell remains
    Long after it's been poured down drains
There's oven cleaner, soda too
    Detergents, just to name a few
Before you rant and make a fuss
    Where does it go when it leaves us
The local river is the place
    To join the fish, like roach or dace
Although it's been through sewage farms
    By means of long revolving arms
And passed through filters, so we hear
    And comes out looking crystal clear
But is it really fit to drink
    That liquid you poured down the sink

It's pumped into the rivers clear
    To mix with what's already there
And some of that's been used before
    When drawn from local reservoir
But some goes out into the sea
    And joins raw sewage, Oh, dear me
The sewage which is discharged raw
    Will sometimes turn up on the shore
And as the tide will ebb and flow
    It doesn't know which way to go
The shellfish which we once enjoyed
    Must be polluted or destroyed
A recent survey now reveals
    Its hideous effect on seals
And what of fish, Cod, Plaice or Huss
    Caught by the ton and sold to us
Evaporation now takes place
    With moisture rising at a pace
It condenses and turns into rain
    And so we get it back again
To use and pour back down the drain

Lew Gray

From My Window

I'd like to see a market place to represent the world
    Where friendship came in wagonloads, and battle flags were
furled
And see it filled with happy folk, with laughter, end to end
    Where no one had an enemy, but everyone a friend
Each stall would offer jars of faith, and bottles filled with hope
    And bundles of assistance, just for those who couldn't cope
With pots and pans of liniment, to satisfy each need
    And barrow loads of lotions, for annihilating greed
Food would all be offered free, and gentleness would thrive
    And friends of every creed would shout, 'It's good to be alive'
Tears would only be allowed, if cried as tears of joy
    But peace would be most commonplace, for each one to enjoy
Charity would come in tubs, with barrels of goodwill
    There'd be no need for anyone to take a bitter pill
There'd be packets of compassion, while others housed the seeds
    Of care, and understanding of other people's needs
Pails would brim with sympathy, the breeze be laced with love
    The sun, the stars, the moon, would bring good tidings from
above
And if modesty became the norm, and vanity was banned
    As Lewis Carroll's walrus said 'Oh, wouldn't that be grand'

Lew Gray

The Ageing Process

Time was when I moved like a cat
Lissom, light, with my feet never flat
But I no longer travel like that
But there, I'm not the type to complain

The change didn't come overnight
It came creeping, insidious, slight
But as certain as day follows night
Or a puddle is formed by light rain

When I found I could not stand the pace
Playing sport, I just bowed out with grace
For I never enjoyed second place
To tell truth, I did not like the pain

With sport we've an option, of course
But look close at the plight of the horse
When they find it's not par for the course
It's just cast to one side with disdain

It will happen to me, that I know
When employers decide I'm too slow
They'll say 'Sorry old chap, you must go'
Perhaps give me a gold watch and chain

Until then I will give it my best
And will try to withstand every test
Then I'll give this old body a rest
And thank God I've been left with a brain
Lew Gray

Children

Does the cry mean I am hungry, or my bum needs tending to?
We really must investigate, who'll do it, me or you?
It could be just a touch of wind, or the nappy could be tight
It's uncanny how it happens in the middle of the night!
Teeth emerge, accompanied by angry cries of pain
Long nights spent pacing bedroom boards, mean broken sleep again
Little face all flushed and spotty, 'Mummy may I have a drink?'
'Mummy, when I don't turn up for school, what will my teacher think?'
'Daddy, may I watch the telly?', 'No, it's time you went to bed'
'But I'm hungry, may I have some jam upon a slice of bread?'
The sound of spits and hisses, quickly followed by a wail
Will tell you that the cat is being carried by its tail
Two scruffy, unkempt figures, both bereft of shoes and socks
Pushing mutilated flower heads in to the rabbit box
My fishing interrupted, 'Daddy, will you help me please
My fishing line has got itself caught up amongst the trees'
'Where do you think you're going?', 'I'm just going out to play'
'You'll stay in and do your homework, your exams aren't far away'
Our youngest son has finished school, he's starting work today
I'ver packed his lunch and seen him off, I hope he'll be O.K.
'Who is this boy you're meeting at the dance on Friday night?'
'You behave yourself, young lady', 'Oh, Mum, I'll be alright'
The neighbours are assembled, each one keen to see the bride
She holds my arm, we walk the aisle, I look at her with pride
How old do children get to be, I had this thought today
It was triggered when my parents came to visit us and stay

My Mother quickly noticed that my collar wasn't straight
Then asked me why I'd left two small potatoes on my plate
Then we had a full inspection of my garden, by my Dad
After criticising several things, he said, 'It's not too bad'
No doubt I've caused them worries, and I hope I've brought them joy
Though I'm wed and have a family, to them I'm still their boy

Lew Gray

Pollution

We used to fish the tidal Ouse, and some folks used to say
That what we did was quite unfair, illegal in a way
We'd drag a bar with sixteen hooks along the river bed
And pull up flounders by the score, and many mouths were fed
We found the fish delicious, in the autumn, full of roe
The locals waited our return, they'd know which days we'd go
I treasure memories of those days we spent out on the boat
Those balmy days of autumn, when we'd never need a coat
I consider we were lucky to have known such carefree days
When we felt we owned the river, and came to know her ways
We never had a single care, and youth was on our side
The only thing that ruled us was the ebb and flow of tide
We loved those days of freedom, and the river was a friend
We took it all for granted, never dreaming it would end
But then we started catching fish with brown and yellow spots
That season there were just a few, the next year there were lots
At first we thought disease had caused the spots upon the fish
And loathed to throw back specimens that should have graced a
dish
But then a word was whispered, which is commonplace today
The whispered word, pollution, and the magic slipped away
Our appetite for fish was gone, enthusiasm waned
And mention of pollution left the conversation strained
Our friend, the river, looked the same, we'd watch it ebb and flow
But when it came to fishing trips, we'd not the heart to go
The boat dried out and crumbled, both the ropes and drag are
gone
Our heads have changed to shades of grey, but the memories live
on
Lew Gray

Farm Sale

He stood inside the stable he had known as man and boy
The wind soughed through the pantiles overhead
And its keening, mournful music made a tear form in his eye
As he called to mind his charges, now long dead

He remembered how they'd whicker, when they heard his heavy tread
As the lantern lit his way across the yard
And the way the mighty Clydesdale always turned his noble head
When he heard the heavy stable door unbarred

They paraded there before him, all the horses he had worked
As his memory strayed and wandered down the years
To him, they were as children, some were willing, others shirked
And if one of them were lost, he'd shed some tears

He recalled the flighty gypsy, with the wild and wicked eye
Who would kick and bite, if given half a chance
And Bruce, the chestnut gelding, requisitioned, and to die
On some crater ridden battlefield in France

There was Tinker, Duke and Boxer, and Diamond and May
And Whitefoot, who would pull with all her heart
And Prince, the mighty Percheron, who'd pull at plough all day
But had a big aversion to the cart

He recalled so many others, he had seen some of them born
He had reared them, taught them all they had to know
He had worked them through the summer's heat when harvesting
the corn
Through showers of spring and even winter's snow

He had held his back against them, so to share their body heat
When he'd paused to eat his bit of bread and cheese
He would give them each an apple, on occasion, as a treat
And they would work as if they wished to please

He stepped into the harness room, surveyed the dismal scene
Of harness strewn in dusty disarray
A room which he had always kept so tidy, neat and clean
Now dusty and infested with decay

The once so sturdy wooden pegs, were in a sorry state
Some had shed their loads onto the floor
Neglect and obsolescence contributed to their fate
As woodworm came to sate its hungry maw

The leather he had cared for, was now green, and cracked, and
dry
Saddles, bridles, martingales and reins
His rounded shoulders trembled, and he gave a weary sigh
As he stroked discoloured brass and rusting chains

In one corner stood a cupboard with a broken, sagging door
One hinge had rusted through and given way
Inside it stood examples of the former horseman's lore
Those closely guarded secrets of his day

He caught a faint aroma of the liniment he'd used
When treating horses for a muscle strain
Some got the strains by accident, while others were abused
When worked by brutes, who had but little brain

He heard the sound of voices, so he made his way outside
To witness people coming to the sale
He noticed several locals, others came from far and wide
Each knew he'd find a bargain without fail

He stood aside and watched them, as they moved among the lines
Of implements he'd used those years ago
Such as ploughs and drills and harrows, and rakes with massive tines
Redundant now, supposedly too slow

He wondered were they really slow? the work was always done
Without the aid of artificial light
Now quicker men, with fast machines, start working with the sun
And rush around 'til half way through the night

He sensed another's presence, so turned aside and saw
A friend, a workmate, master, in one man
Their ageing hands gripped warmly, as they'd often done before
When schemes they'd plotted worked out to the plan

84

They had started school together, where they'd learned, and
laughed and vied
For honours, and played cricket for the team
They had learned their trade together, working hard, and side by
side
Each held the other one in high esteem

Although they had worked together they were really poles apart
One had the role of master, one of man
But it really didn't matter, for they seemed to share one heart
As only those who've worked together can

Each one had known the other would attend the sale that day
For one last look at all the tools they'd used
When ploughing, cultivating, drilling seed, or turning hay
Most of them now outdated and unused

Then the bidding started, first a pile of rusting scrap
Which had gathered in odd corners down the years
Atop it lay the metal from a broken pony trap
Whose sad demise had brought both blood and tears

The trap was on a journey into town one market day
When it collided with a lorry, on a bend
The trap was being driven by the farmer's daughter, May
She fell beneath the wheels and met her end

The auctioneer continued, taking bids from all around
The people milled and moved along the rows
Of sundry tools, in numbered lots, laid out upon the ground
Such as shovels, spades, and rakes, and forks and hoes

The auctioneer called loudly, 'This is lot two twenty eight
An hermaphrodite, who'll bid me fifty quid?'
The two friends looked it over, it was in a sorry state
They stared in disbelief when someone did

They smiled at one another, when somebody bought the plough
They had wrestled with, that never would run straight
It had caused them both to sweat and swear and work with fur-
rowed brow
And silently they bid him, 'Good luck mate!'

Somebody bought a tractor he intended to restore
Another, a machine for dressing corn
Nobody seemed to want an old machine for cutting straw
Or a binder, sails askew and canvas torn

The type of items offered, changed as progress made its mark
And tractors ousted horses from the scene
A crawler tractor, rigged with lights for ploughing after dark
A tractor hoe which bore the name of Bean

A kaleidoscope of implements were offered, one by one
An ambidextrous plough, a heavy roll
A manure spreader, built to hold a quarter of a ton
An implement for drainage, called a mole

A Peter Standen harvester, for lifting sugar beet
A standard Fordson, iron clad all round
An early tractor, called a Case, which hadn't any seat
A chisel plough for breaking heavy ground

And so the sale continued, 'til the final lot was sold
Business had been brisk, the bidding keen
The sale had been of interest to all, both young and old
But now they slowly drifted from the scene

Though some were very busy, loading up the things they'd
bought
Onto lorries, trailers, carts and vans and such
Some happy with the price they'd paid for the items they had
sought
While others moaned, and said they'd paid too much

Although they'd watched in silence, they were happy in a way
Their memories rekindled by the sale
The two friends took one final look, then turned and walked away
And headed to the pub to have some ale

Lew Gray 1996

Hannah

Our Hannah had to fight for life, right from the very start
For scans had shown she had a massive problem with her heart
We took her to Great Ormond Street, they said they'd operate
But first we had to take her home, to gain both strength and weight

But Hannah didn't gain in weight, she looked so weak and frail
Her condition simply worsened as her heart began to fail
We took her into Rudham Ward, that's at the QE2
And those dedicated people did the best that they could do

They balanced this and juggled that, they put her on a drip
And Hannah clung to life you know, would not relax her grip
We then received a message from Great Ormond Street, which read
She'll have to wait another week, we haven't got a bed

We counted down the hours, indeed, we lived in dread
We thought, if they don't operate our Hannah will be dead
But the staff of Rudham Ward fought hard, and kept our girl alive
The day arrived, Great Ormond Street, a good two hour drive

Then we met that brilliant team, who'd planned what they would do
They introduced another, whom they said was passing through
He asked would we allow him to assist and help them out
He had some new equipment, which had barely been tried out

We'd discussed our Hannah's chances, we were told they weren't good
And so we asked the man to give them all the help he could

So that brilliant group of people carried out the work they'd planned
And we're ceetain that an angel came and held our Hannah's hand
She survived the operation, went into Intensive Care
For days and nights she fought for life, with always someone there

She was heavily sedated, she had tubes and pipes and all
They sucked out rubbish from her lungs, but couldn't reach it all
Despite all this attention, Hannah couldn't get her breath
We could but stare in horror, she was very close to death

But with one almighty effort, Hannah coughed up blood and gore
The experts were astounded, scarce believing what they saw
That seemed to be the turning point, our girl was on the mend
And everyone who helped our girl, we think of as a friend

We thank them from our hearts, for all those days and night they toiled
Then came that magic moment, Hannah looked at us and smiled
We went back to the QE2 and into Rudham Ward
The staff all gathered round and saw our little girl restored

They cared for her for four more days, our Hannah was a star
Then we were told to take her home, we put her in the car
Now our Hannah's getting better, and we thank God for the day
Of our Hannah's operation, when an agel walked her way

Lew Gray

Trapped

They come to the country from city or town
To purchase the house of their dreams
With the contract signed up, the for sale notice down
They are perfectly happy, it seems

Well, not perfectly happy, there's things to put right
That wallpaper is wrong, for a start
That paintwork won't do it's a hideous sight
And that fireplace is not very smart

Just look at the garden, it's covered in weeds
We shall have to do something with that
The dyke at the bottom is full of Fen weeds
And that boy down the road is a brat

So we'll concrete the garden, yes, that's the best thing
And we'll pull up that hedgerow as well
And as for that Farmer, I'll give him a ring
Corse those pigs that he keeps doan arf smell

Why does the wind have to blow, day and night
Or those wood pigeons wake us at dawn
No wonder it's dark, not a street lamp in sight
And those insects must thrive in that corn

We can't have a knees up on Saturday night
Corse that Landlord's a bit of a burk
And as for those locals, they're not very bright
They call in the pub straight from work

Whatever possessed us, we must have been mad
To come here at the end of this track
Yes, we made a bad move, and the future looks bad
For we cannot afford to go back

Lew Gray

Head Piece

Small fishes swim from sockets where once eyes
Looked out eagerly to scan the war torn skies
The skies that hid the cannon from a plane
That ruptured flesh, broke bones and pulped the brain
The brain that thought, as many had before
That only other people died in war
The war that seemed so very far away
From cosy cockpit on that sunny day
That sunny day that could have been enjoyed
Had not the bombs and bullets been deployed
Deployed by men of unrelenting greed
Used by puppets who could never share that need
That need to own what other people had
A feeling so intense, it drove them mad
Mad enough to organise a war
And push the common people to the fore
Fore, came the cry from Berlin, London Rome
And caused this skull to be a fish's home

Lew Gray 1995

Art Gallery

Folks' artistic talents on display
Colours garish, gentle, every hue
Methwold Church portrayed by J.P. Gray
Its lancelike steeple spears a sky of blue

A spitfire dressed in wartime camouflage
A barn owl sets out on its nightly hunt
Sunset silhouettes a broadland barge
A moorhen's nest close by a rotting punt

A dormouse dines on fallen flower seeds
A bramble's thorns protect its luscious fruits
A warbler's nest suspended in the reeds
A pair of kittens groom their furry suits

A flint, used as an anvil by a thrush
All this, and more, for everyone to see
By people who are skilled with paint and brush
Light, colour, shade and line in symmetry

I envy those whose hand and eye combine
But realise I must not be deterred
For though their precious gift cannot be mine
I'll try to capture scenes with rhyme and word

Lew Gray

Danny Dragon Lights The Way

Russet Reindeer rang round his relations
Who were scattered far and wide, held many stations
He said 'I can't remember
When we last met in December
To partake of the Christmas celebrations'

Russet said, in his opinion, they
Should meet up for the Christmas holiday
They very soon agreed
'Twas a splendid plan indeed
Apart from one, whose answer would be 'Nay'

Poor Rudolph was the one who couldn't come
He'd be too busy helping out his chum
He'd be lighting up the way
For Father Christmas and his sleigh
So Rudolph put the 'phone down, feeling glum

Then Rudolph moped, his countenance was grim
A trait which was unusual for him
He was in a gloomy mood
And he went right off his food
And the light within his nose grew very dim

But Father Christmas is astute and kind
And seemingly he read young Rudolph's mind
He said 'Cheer up, old lad
Things can't really be so bad
So smile, and put this misery behind'

Then Rudolph sniffed and wore a worried frown
Saying, 'I must light your way to every town
To deliver all the toys
To all the girls and boys
Or you'll get lost, we cannot let them down'

Then Father Christmas said 'It's been the norm
For you to light my way through any storm
But I'm sure young Danny Dragon
Who drinks brandy by the flagon
Will light my way and also keep me warm'

'I've taken you for granted, dear old friend
I didn't realise you wished to spend
This Christmas with relations
For the season's celebrations
So off you go, and here's some cash to spend'

Then Rudolph smiled and gave a happy yell
The light within his nose lit up as well
So he 'phoned his cousin Russ
And said 'I'm coming on the bus
To join you at the Reindeers' Rest Hotel!'

Lew Gray

Forward Planning

Those years ago, when we had slaves
And many went to early graves
Great Britain took an early stand
Declaring slavery is banned

Then someone had a new idea, which proved to be a gem
We leave the slaves in situ now, and send the work to them

Lew Gray

A Boyhood Fenland Sunday

I woke to hear the primus heating water for the tea
And Father raking cinders from the grate
I turned the bedclothes back and put my feet down cautiously
It was almost ten past five, and I was late

The flashlight flickered round the room, the lino chilled my feet
My Brother stirred, then gave a gentle snore
I quickly dressed, for Sunday breakfast was a special treat
Then left the room and quietly closed the door

I walked into the kitchen where the fire was flaring bright
The table lamp threw shadows on the wall
My boots stood on the fender, where they dried out through the
night
I put them on, I had to make a call

I visited the toilet which stood fifty yards away
Then let the Labrador free from his chain
I heard a distant cockerel as he heralded the day
The cloud hung low, I hoped it wouldn't rain

I walked up to a ferret box, no sound came from within
Until I ran my fingers down the wire
The sleeping quarters rumbled 'midst a snarling, squeaking din
Then eyes appeared, some glowed like orbs of fire

I fetched two pails of water from the tap out by the gate
So Mother wouldn't have to do that chore
Then washed my hands, as Father piled my breakfast on my plate
I ate the lot, and could have eaten more

With breakfast cooked and eaten, we then headed for the shed
The cats arrived, both eager for a feed
As Father held the lantern, I mixed up the milk and bread
Then we sorted the equipment we would need

A most essential tool would be the lightweight digging spade
Then the digging staff with handle six feet long
And nets and stakes and string, all of the rabbit catcher's trade
Two guns would also have to come along

One ferret lived a lonely life, apart from all the rest
The lantern lit his coat of cream and grey
He didn't try to bite me, he just nibbled me in jest
A killer who just felt the need to play

The sky toward the east began to show a yellow stain
As we sorted ferrets, casting some aside
The vicious, odd eyed hybrid tried to bite me once again
He missed, I picked him up, he glared and sighed

The ferrets were all eager, but we didn't need them all
And some of them had worked on Saturday
And one we couldn't use because he had a nasty gall
We got them boxed, we'd soon be on our way

We went back to the house, to get the food we'd need to take
Bread and dripping, sausage rolls and currant buns
I slipped into the kitchen, pinched a slice of home made cake
While Father fetched the cartridges and guns

It was nearly ten to seven when we picked up all our stuff
And between us we had quite a heavy load
We had more than a mile to go, the going would be rough
As soon as we were forced to leave the road

We passed a row of bungalows, their windows curtained, dark
It seemed to me the world was still abed
Then somewhere in the distance, someone's dog began to bark
We concentrated on the road ahead

We reached the point to leave the road, and crossed a stowaway
Then walked along a furrow, straight and true
We slipped and slid around a bit, this field was mostly clay
Which gathered on our boots, and stuck like glue

We had to walk a greasy plank to get across a drain
With murky water lurking there below
This ancient plank would always creak and bend beneath the strain
I always half expected it to go

As we crossed a field of stubble, which stood waiting for the plough
A pheasant leapt and rocketed away
We must have caught him sleeping, we surprised him anyhow
And he shouted his indignance at the day

We walked across the headland of a field of winter wheat
And came up to a heavy five barred gate
We paused to scrape the heavy, sticky mud off of our feet
And were very pleased to shed the extra weight

100

The Labrador was happy, as we walked his favourite patch
He hunted back and forth, which was the norm
He knew from former trips, there might be something here to catch
And he soon picked up a rabbit from a form

We came up to the stockyard, nestled close beside a bank
The cattle stirred on hearing us approach
A heron lifted from the drain, and raucously cried fraank
It sounded like a message of reproach

The cattle were all hungry, and the water tanks were dry
Forty thirsty mouths had drunk the lot
The pump I'd have to fill them with, to me, was shoulder high
And the filter would get choked with weed and cot

I climbed down to the filter, and cleaned it best I could
Then Father came to help me prime the pump
It was ancient, worn and leaky, for the seals weren't over good
It was fastened to a massive bog oak stump

It took us several minutes just to get the pump to prime
But then I felt the water start to flow
I decided I would try to fill the tanks in record time
But had several hundred gallons left to go

The cattle crowded round the tanks, sucked water greedily
Ten minutes passed, the tanks were empty still
I knew the score, I settled down and pumped resignedly
I wouldn't gain until they'd had their fill

I continued pumping water, Father fed them pulp and chaff
The cattle crowded, eager to be fed
One of them trod on Father's foot, I simply had to laugh
His language would have baked a loaf of bread

Three quarters of an hour passed, I daren't have a rest
I'd have lost the prime we'd worked for if I had
I wouldn't break my record, but I'd given it my best
The tanks were almost full and I was glad

Now the cattle needed mangolds, they'd eat half a ton or more
We had to pitch the mangolds through a hole
Then I had to spread the mangolds out, while Father pitched them straw
It seemed to me we'd never reach our goal

But then we had it finished and we gathered up our gear
The Labrador was instantly awake
He led the way, with Father next, while I brought up the rear
A breeze picked up, the cloud began to break

The Labrador flushed moorhen from some willows by a pond
They didn't leap, but lumbered into flight
He then chased snipe from clumps of sedge, of which they're very fond
And I'm certain it was done with great delight

Another forty cattle waited, half a mile ahead
Their distant bawling carried loud and clear
They milled inside the railings, each one eager to be fed
And the noise intensified as we drew near

We only had to feed and straw, the water was on tap
And a ball valve in the tank controlled the flow
But first we had to pause to take a rabbit from a trap
Of the type so rightly banned those years ago

Then Father carted pulp and chaff, I cut and pitched the straw
And littered it around to form a bed
Onto which we pitched the mangolds, through an elevated door
And just an hour later, they were fed

We ate our bread and dripping, drank some Bettox from a flask
The Labrador sat waiting for a crust
He had spent the morning sleeping, while we stuck to our task
So for him to share our dockey seemed unjust

Then we had to coop the ferrets, so they couldn't bite, just nip
With special strings prepared the night before
It was vital that we tied them so they couldn't get a grip
So that they could only threaten, nip and claw

We didn't want the rabbits killed, we wanted them to run
If killed, we'd have to dig them from their holes
We preferred to catch them in a net, or shoot them with a gun
And hoped to leave the digging to the moles

Most ferrets didn't struggle, they had all been cooped before
Though one or two of them played up a bit
The vicious, odd eyed hybrid slashed my finger with a claw
And I wasn't over pleased, I must admit

We walked up to a burrow, stepping softly as we could
Then strung a net some fifty yards ahead
The Labrador sat statue like, as if he understood
That silence now would stand us in good stead

We slipped the ferrets down the holes, they eagerly complied
And quickly disappeared below the ground
We took up our positions, so we covered either side
Two minutes passed, we never heard a sound

Then we heard a rumble and a rabbit streaked away
Father fired a shot and it lay dead
Another rabbit bolted and my gun came into play
I missed, the rabbit carried on ahead

I was pleased to see it running straight, it could have veered away
To quickly disappear into a dyke
It held its course, and so it brought the long net into play
And some would say it wasn't sportsmanlike

We never thought of it as sport, we needed meat to eat
And anything left over, we could sell
For meat was still on ration, so a rabbit was a treat
We dried, and sold the rabbit skins as well

My reverie was halted by a shot from Father's gun
A rabbit rolled, he'd made another kill
He fired again, unerringly, and killed another one
And all the while, the Labrador sat still

Several hectic minutes followed, rabbits bolted left and right
Gunsmoke, fur and pellets filled the air
Father killed another three, some disappeared from sight
And I was quite relieved to bag a pair

Ferrets started reappearing, so I laid my shotgun down
Then picked the ferrets up and cleaned their feet
But one of them did not appear, this caused us both to frown
We had to dig, we hoped it would be fleet

The ferret who lived on his own, would have to earn his keep
I fixed the leather collar round his neck
He blinked his eyes as if to clear away four hours' sleep
I fixed his line, on which we'd keep a check

This ferret, who we called Big Bob, had quite a job to do
He had to find that ferret underground
'Midst a myriad of tunnels he would have to hunt them through
Then chase the ferret out, once he was found

That ferret wouldn't argue, when Big Bob came on the scene
He would quickly scuttle off to find the light
He wouldn't argue with a stranger, who was open mouthed and
mean
In a tunnel which was darker than the night

Bob searched a half a dozen holes, but each one was in vain
He'd search away, until the line ran out
When this happened, he'd return to me again
For he knew what this business was about

The line was only ten yards long, the burrow twice as long
We had to search it systematically
So when a hole proved fruitless, it would simply move along
We'd track that ferret down eventually

Big Bob searched another hole, the line jumped through my hand
I knew what we had searched for had been found
The ferret with the coop on had appeared, just as we planned
He seemed quite pleased to be above the ground

Father boxed the wayward ferret, while I tended to the line
Big Bob was busy just four yards ahead
The line jumped through my fingers which I took to be a sign
That the rabbit Bob was with would soon be dead

I looked down at the line and was delighted when I saw
Four knots which placed Big Bob four yards ahead
We wouldn't dig a trench, oh no, we didn't need that chore
Far better to dig single holes instead

Father put the gun aside, picked up the digging spade
Peeled off the turf three feet ahead of me
Then changed it for the digging staff which had a narrow blade
So would cut down through the earth more easily

Earth fell on the line, then Father turned the staff around
Then used the metal hook to probe below
His efforts were rewarded, and the line was quickly found
We'd gained a yard and had three more to go

As Father dug the final hole, he did it cautiously
We knew Big Bob must be there, close at hand
He'd done his job and made our job much easier you see
And things had turned out just the way we'd planned

Suddenly the earth gave way, and then we saw Big Bob
Father hooked the line, I pulled it through
Then cleaned the fur from Big Bob's claws, for he had done his job
As for us, we'd still a lot to do

We then enlarged the hole, and soon I pulled a rabbit out
That one was followed by another three
We knew it was our lucky day, of that there was no doubt
Our catch would soon be turned to £ S D

The net which we'd deployed had carried out its deadly work
Four rabbits struggled, trying to break free
But Father quickly broke their necks with just a single jerk
The stowing of the net was left to me

We collected all the rabbits, were delighted with the count
Twenty seven rabbits was the score
In the past we'd had good catches, but never that amount
I must admit, it thrilled me to the core

Father said 'Don't get excited, just put this down to luck
And think about some leaner days we've had
Of days when we have struggled hard and barely broke our duck
And gone home disappointed, tired and sad'

We filled in all the holes we'd dug and packed the earth down
tight
Young horses grazed this bank wheb summer came
For them, holes would spell danger as they move around at night
And if one got hurt, we didn't want the blame

Father hulked and legged the rabbits, as I quickly dug a hole
Our golden rule was bury all the waste
We didn't want to feed some hungry fox out on patrol
Or allow those feral cats to get a taste

The journey home was looming and I shuddered at the thought
I thought the journey out was hard enough
But now we had the weight of all the rabbits we had caught
Father said the exercise would make me tough

As we started out for home, we had a final look around
It always paid to have that final check
That we hadn't left some vital piece of gear there on the ground
Three rabbits on a string hung round my neck

The Labrador seemed sated as we walked a muddy drov e
It seemed he'd lost the urge to hunt and roam
I'll swear I caught a whiff of dinner cooking on the stove
And we were still a half a mile from home

It was almost ten past three when we arrived back at our gate
And Mother brought us each a mug of tea
She looked me up and down and said 'Your clothes are in a state
It seems you thrive on making work for me'

We cleaned, then fed the ferrets, and this caused a great furore
They fought for every bit with tooth and claw
Mother came across the yard and fed the Labrador
He gulped it down and looked around for more

As we cleaned the digging spade and staff, picked rubbish from
the net
The smell of cooking wafted on the air
I thought, that smells a lot like stew, I wonder what we've got
But hungry as I was, I didn't care

My brother came and told us Mother's serving up the food
That we should come and eat it while it's hot
We'd worked up quite an appetite, and so were in the mood
To savour stew and dumplings from the pot

The pot contained four pigeons, mixed with vegetables galore
With Norfolk dumplings steaming on the top
I cleared my plate, and Mother smiled, she knew I'd want some
more
Bread soaked the juice, I didn't waste a drop

When the meal was over we went back out to the shed
Ten rabbits had been ordered for that night
Three of them needed skinning, well that's what the people said
While Father did the job, I held the light

We charged the people sixpence to remove a rabbit skin
The scrap man gave us fourpence for each one
Some people would have wasted them, and thrown them in the
bin
They bought us ammunition for the gun

Father tidied up the rabbits and placed them in a sack
I checked my bike, made sure the tyres were hard
The front light shone, but there was just a glimmer from the back
I'd have to chance my luck, be on my guard

When I checked the list from Mother, I was very pleased to see
That three deliveries were in our row
I did those three on foot, which was much easier for me
Which meant I'd only seven more to go

I set out on the bike, another seven calls to make
Kind faces greeted me at every door
One lady fed me sausage rolls, another home made cake
I'd brought the meat they'd all been hoping for

They knew we couldn't guarantee that we'd supply the meat
Luck would always play a major part
And with butcher's meat on ration, a wild rabbit was a treat
It made a lovely pie, or stew, or tart

One lady said she didn't have the extra cash for me
The rabbit had been skinned at her request
She said she'd pay in kind, and handed me a pack of tea
Then said 'It's Brooke Bond Divi, it's the best'

The sack was almost empty as I reached the final drop
They greeted me with warmth, said 'Come in lad'
Then I placed two rabbits on the kitchen table top
At last the job was done, and I was glad

The lady said 'What's going on, I only ordered one
You know full well, we've never wanted two'
The man said 'Blame your Father, it's his way of having fun
When I meet him I shall tell him what to do'

I put the spare one in the sack then headed for Hell Row
Assisted by a cool, but gentle, breeze
But with the journey's end in sight, and not too far to go
The local Bobby stepped out from the trees

He snatched the sack away from me and turned it upside down
The rabbit fell, and landed in the grass
He said 'This must be mine'. I said 'It is, for half a crown'
He said 'Go home before I kick your arse'

As soon as I got home I told them all that had transpired
That the local Bobby owed us half a crown
But Father smiled and said that it was just what we required
I didn't understand, it made me frown

He said 'I'd best explain to you, there's much you need to learn
About the way us Fenland people live
In time you'll find that life will throw up many a twist and turn
Sometimes we take, sometimes we have t o give

I guessed you'd be confronted by the Constable tonight
That he would know where we had been today
And you would be fair game, because you hadn't a rear light
A nice fresh rabbit might turn things our way

And so the plan has worked, though it was simple in design
It really did work well, yes, just the job
Had he issued you a summons, then it would have meant a fine
Which, at the very least, would be five bob'

Mother counted up the money, then took the pack of tea
Inspected it close by the table lamp
She turned it in her fingers, then she smiled and said to me
'That old sod has kept the divi stamp'

I went into the wash house, where the fire was just aglow
The water in the copper was still warm
I stripped my clothes, then had a thorough wash from head to toe
Then dressed in clean, warm clothes, which was the norm

When I went back to the kitchen, Father sat there cleaning guns
My Brother ran his train set on the floor
I said to Mother 'Have you made a batch of currant buns?'
She smiled and opened up the oven door

She pulled out baked potatoes which had been cooked to a turn
Majestics, on which we had won the war
Sliced open, they were spread with butter from a local churn
Sadly, the Majestics are no more

Father opened up the oven, then pulled two house bricks out
Mother brought some cloths to wrap each one
We quickly put them on our bed, we didn't hang about
We knew they'd not been warmed up just for fun

Father said' 'It's after nine o'clock, it's time you went to bed'
I helped my Brother put his train away
Mother took the cats outside and shut them in the shed
We said 'Goodnight' and went our weary way

Snug, tired and warm beneath the clothes, I started counting sheep
Proud that I had withstood evey test
One question left unanswered as I drifted into sleep
What fool said Sunday was a day of rest!

Forty Years of Marriage

We met in Three Holes village hall at a Country and Western
dance
It must have been fate that took me along, for I hadn't a clue how
to dance

When the dance ended I saw Beryl home, but 'twas not in a fancy
sports car
Between us we had just a couple of bikes, but no matter 'twas not
very far

After that we would meet up at every weekend and on Wednes-
day night, if we could
We got on so well and I thought to myself, the future looks rosy
and good

Then we progressed to an old B.S.A. and how Beryl coped I don't
know
In summer we'd ride amongst warm oil and flies and in winter,
rain, ice and snow

But it meant we could go to the pictures in March, or in Down-
ham or Lynn
And no matter the weather, we'd always turn out and sometimes
get soaked to the skin

Or we might run the gauntlet of Wisbech among Teddy Boys,
Vanners and Yanks
But we'd always emerge from the melee unscathed, or we'd pic-
nic on lush grassy banks

Then I had to go into the forces, to serve Queen and country you
know
We had bullshit and drill, and the food was like swill, and the pay
was exceedingly low

Then I was told I'd been placed on a draft, to go to the States, so
they said
We thought marriage allowance would bolster our funds, and
decided to quickly get wed

We were wed under special licence, the village tongues wagged
merrily
They were certain that Beryl was pregnant, but we both knew dif-
ferent you see

We were wed at the Wesleyan Chapel, where they posted a guard
at the door
Because Beryl was late and I was irate, but I knew she was worth
waiting for

In the winter that spanned sixty two, sixty three, we were living
in Marshland Fen
Where we'd wake with our breath turned to ice on the sheets, but
people were hardier then

Well we haven't moved far, but we've come a long way and it's
just forty years to the day
When we went to the chapel in Nordelph, and Sid gave his
daughter away

Yes it's been forty years, 'what a sentence', if only someone
would explain
Why some infamous people did ten years less, and that was for
robbing a train

You know Beryl has led such an unselfish life, and although some
events have been sad
She has taken good care of both me and the boys, and has nursed
both her mum and her dad

Yes, Beryl has been such a wonderful wife, and I know for a fact
you'll agree
She truly deserves the George Medal for her forty years living
with me

Lew Gray